PART OF IT

1705302719

THE CON STARTS WITH THIS:
'What it is . . . '
Which is what it isn't.
I'm on Whitworth Street in the centre of Manchester, England. I've been accosted by a casually dressed 30-something man with a pronounced Mancunian accent who's about to tell me 'what it is'.

What it 'is' is a convoluted tale of a car that has run out of petrol on Tibb Street (close enough to be vaguely plausible, too far away to readily verify); a mobile phone that is dead (vague illustrative gesture with said prop here); a mother and sister who couldn't be reached as tonight is their darts night; and a request to be helped out with a few pounds, which my narrator will, like he says, pay back — he's just stuck.

What it also 'is' is a frequently performed dance — a crude but effective choreography of well-rehearsed combinations to implicate an unwilling partner. The man I encounter has refined just such a set of blitz tactics into a highly efficient subroutine:[1]

---

1 In the heyday of one of the many subcultures of New York's Washington Square Park, it was said that one of the speed-chess players there could often beat a Grand Master at this version of the game, because the one-second tempo of this brute outline of the game precluded subtlety, fractal thought, etc., and allowed only the broadest patterns of play to develop. Quick kills, forestalling strategic counters. 'Putz chess', as the affcionados would sniff, but effective.

I

1   Politely acknowledge the assumptions about private space the
    victim makes within the city, even as you intrude on it with
    your salutation.

2   Maintain a running commentary as you hijack their criteria for
    moving and engaging in the city.

3   With body, word and tempo, quickly close down the social arena
    as a boxer would the ring, preventing escape.

4   Further forestall any protest by moving swiftly to a request, which
    also functions as a claim about what is being transacted between
    you — the price the victim must pay for extraction is now at the
    very least a counter claim.

5   If challenged or refused at any point, drop the fiction fast and
    walk away. Press, harry and maintain a forced tension, yes, but
    never overreach.

6   Go to 1.

What it is then is a generic set of moves, phrases and choreographies that
can be encountered in cities worldwide — though, like all such apparently
modular solutions for delinquent living, it still reflects local idiosyncrasies.
The encounter takes place outside India House, a former warehouse on a
street of warehouses in a compact Victorian city centre. We're near the point
where Whitworth Street and Oxford Road intersect — a popular crossroads
marked on respective corners by, at the time of this incident, Cornerhouse
Arts Centre (by Oxford Road Railway Station), a subterranean bar called

Copper Face Jacks,[2] the Palace Theatre and a new 'warehouse-style' apartment complex. Despite the prominence of these streets on city maps, they are narrow — relics of the industrial revolution's accompanying civic ambivalence in Manchester — conspicuous consumption at the level of the newly-minted private citizen, coupled with a reticence at encountering those whose labour created that wealth. Hence narrow arterial routes to the city centre, once lined with rows of shops disguising slums, like so many flimsy theatrical flats, most notably in the case of Little Ireland (made infamous by Friedrich Engels' *The Condition of the Working Class in England*), the remains of which are maybe 400 yards from where we stand. These narrow streets create natural bottlenecks on busy corners — ripe for interventions, the present-day arts centre, playhouse and train station ensure a flow of transient targets, emerging on predictable ebbs and flows of entertainment schedules, licensing laws and transportation timetables. Retold on this corner, the same story can encounter shifting sets of audiences.

Further revealing qualities of space are apparent. This is the third time in as many months I've come across a variation on this story within 30 yards of my front door (my friends have coined a term to describe the phenomenon — 'The Petrol Liars'). There has been a recent intensifying of these incidents.

---

2 Site of one of my favourite photographs, by Manchester artist Jim Medway, showing the traffic light on this corner covered with small balls of chewing gum. The bar was in the basement of the Refuge Assurance building (now the Palace Hotel) and had proved a troublesome spot to fill over the years, as people weren't necessarily sure it was there. The tight corner left little room for street signage, so doormen would be dispatched to serve in an ambivalent attract/repel mode. Their black bomber jackets and burly presence would signify the entrance to the bar and attract prospective patrons, who would then face the whims of the bouncer-as-filter. More often than not the doormen would be left unoccupied and unchallenged with only each other and an endless supply of gum for company. In his essay 'Signs on Stones', Primo Levi discusses the staying power of discarded chewing gum — noting that following the density of its pattern in city streets will inevitably lead to a bar or restaurant or some site of human concentration, as surely as the shark finds prey by following drops of blood in the water. When I look at this image I imagine an elaborate act of forestalling within the 'theatre of the street' — some criminal auteur's fanciful collusion with the doorman and bar management to increase the appearance of population density and flow at that corner, by faking the traces and window-dressing the con.

A little more context on this: at one point in the early 1990s only a few hundred people lived within a couple of square miles of Manchester's city centre.
Subsequent events were hardly atypical for former industrial cities adjusting to
a new globalising reality — adjustments mostly marked by an assertion of a
largely mythical historical coherence for those centres.[3] To some, this seemed like
nothing so much as a return to the logic of the medieval city and by extension its
walls of containment, exclusion and selective tolerance[4] — though the passionate
advocates of these developments would more likely invoke the idea of the pulsing
network hub on a larger decentralised network. The liberation rhetoric of the
advocates of the web found much favour with those in British provincial cities who
felt slighted by the metrocentric exercising of power at the level of national politics.

---

3 David Harvey has described this process — the paradox whereby the capitalist urge to seek
   new markets ends up placing locally branded products within an ever-wider and yet more
   homogenous field of competition and then finds itself having to reassert the parochial authenticity (an intensified authenticity at that) of the *genius loci* of the product to differentiate the
   product and protect the market share. A particularly pertinent example might be Boddingtons
   beer belatedly playing off its status as 'The Cream of Manchester' in the 1990s.

4 The obvious example is the 'liberties' region of London in the early modern era — a marginal
   area extending up to three miles from the ancient Roman wall of the city and serving both a
   symbolic and material role within the overall economy and rule of law of the city. The liberties
   belonged to the city in one sense — sharing its name and circulations of population, but as ter-
   rains they were 'at liberty' from obligations to the crown — outside of the jurisdiction of the
   mayor, sheriffs, etc. In a geopolitical sense they were marginalised, yet they were entirely central to the economic and social function and image of the city. The modern-day civic repurposing of areas that were once central business districts for residential purposes has to play off a
   similar ambivalence as symbolism is retooled alongside infrastructure — to be coherent in its
   new claims for itself, the redesigned centre needs to also reinvent and rename its edges.

5 Anderton achieved the status of folk-devil in Manchester — amongst other things he was the
   putative inspiration for the Happy Mondays song 'God's Cop'.

6 There were two particularly prominent examples. First, the continued harassment of
   Manchester publishers Savoy Books, whose *Meng and Ecker* comics (named after a staid, long-
   running post-war Manchester café) became the subject of an obscenity trial. Also, a novel by the
   comic's author, David Britton, *Lord Horror*, became the first novel to be banned in Britain since

In the case of Manchester's physical city centre, an abundance of warehouse building stock and a long post-war decline had left a landscape of sooty redbrick, vacant lots and ill-considered 1960s transport and shopping hubs. In echoes of the medieval version of events, they were presided over by a tyrannic police chief, James Anderton,[5] whose interventions extended into everything from licensing (a strict cap existed on new pub licenses in the city centre – ensuring a healthy secondary private market in selling what should have cost a few pounds) to censorship.[6] When Anderton was forced into retirement in 1991 (in the wake of embarrassing revelations about the ironic behaviour of his much-vaunted vice squad in the course of their 'battles with monsters') the face of the city began to change dramatically. The gay, and then straight, club-and-pub

---

Hubert Selby Jr.'s *Last Exit to Brooklyn* was banned in 1968. In Anderton's first five years as police chief, the publishers were raided more than 40 times. In the other infamous case, Eastern Bloc record shop, at that point in the middle of its brief tenure as the hippest record shop in the world for its role in the 'Madchester' scene, was raided and charged with displaying 'obscene articles for publication for gain'. The shop had been selling the album *The Fucking Cunts Treat Us Like Pricks* by the anarcho-punk group A Flux of Pink Indians. The latter case caused the more immediate public furore, though is perhaps less lovingly documented online now – Savoy always had a keen eye on self-consciously archiving its position within a literary heritage of sub-version (its name was taken from the infamous *fin-de-siècle* magazine *The Savoy*) and their current website wears their ongoing persecution as a badge of pride. Eastern Bloc, despite at the time being positioned within a quasi-formal networked 'cartel' of post-punk independent record shops, was arguably less interested in the significance of the case for others and place little claim to it in their current incarnation of online music warehousing – in true Mancunian tradition (the tradition of warehousing, that is, rather than the other more patchy ongoing streak of civic radicalism). Retrieving the respective digital traces of these two delinquent, analogue histories is an uncanny experience for me – my personal memories of these local disturbances of vinyl and paper are interspersed with images of fixed telephone landlines in communal student halls and of selective information in plastic-wrapped books physically carried from E.Vincent Harris's 1934 Central Library building – the friction of the physical world intruding persistently. So retrieving digital versions of these memories out of the meta-archive now serves to unbalance me – like pulling a cork that's actually resting on the lip of a bottle. Somewhere between the imbalance of this current moment of narration and the pre-Ecstasy dead weight of Anderton's Manchester is the transitive (and transient) moment I meet the liar.

scene flourished with a wave of café-bars opening. 'London Docklands/Dublin Temple Bar/Barcelona Olympic-style' development became the rage and with that came a wave of warehouse conversions for the now-burgeoning city-centre population. When the useable stock for this latter process reached saturation point, the council imposed a moratorium on future conversion development on the remaining listed Victorian warehouses — kick-starting a wave of new-build developments in ersatz warehouse styles.

This brings us back to the fourth corner of the intersection of Oxford and Whitworth Streets. Since the 1970s the lot had been vacant — the residual walls of the demolished St. Mary's Hospital had latterly bounded an unpaved car park often used by the cars and coaches of the patrons visiting the Palace Theatre across the street.[7] As per the typical flow of wealth and traffic in the city, these visitors would largely arrive from the affluent south of the city or the suburbs that gave way to the rich county of Cheshire (as the Victorian merchants had done before them). They would undoubtedly have been glad about the convenient access to the theatre, albeit with the minor risk of a trip-and-fall over the remaining fragments of rubble.

As Whitworth Street underwent a resurgence in the 1990s, the lot became prime property. So it was with some inevitability that the W3 'loft-style' apartments eventually shot up to loom over this corner and compound the structural bottleneck at this city junction. A generic luxury-apartment development for those seeking the thrills of city centre living, the W3 building also ensured that an additional few hundred yards was now added to the average theatregoer's commute to the Palace.

---

7 'St. Mary's Hospital and Dispensary for the diseases peculiar to women and also for the diseases of children under six years of age', to give it its full title, had led a peripatetic existence around the city — at one point existing as the 'Manchester Lying-in Hospital and Charity for the delivery of poor women at their own habitation' in the premises of a former inn in Salford — the bar serving as the matron's room (John J. Parkinson-Bailey, *Manchester: An Architectural History*, 2000). The W3 building that has replaced it has a top-heavy presence that feels paradoxically intrusive and insubstantial, with the overall impression being that of a structure no more destined for permanence than its predecessor, no matter how big a shadow the façade might cast.

At one time Manchester had the most theatres outside London – particularly music halls tied to the bread-and-circus techniques of emergent industrial capitalism.[8] The Palace Theatre had been built with loftier aspirations (opening with a production of *Cleopatra* in 1891) – though it swiftly settled into a populist programme in the early twentieth-century and enjoyed a period of sustained success in doing so. Performers such as Gracie Fields, Laurel and Hardy, Noel Coward and Judy Garland all made appearances there. By the time the hospital across the street was torn down in the early 1970s, though, attendances were down and the theatre itself faced closure. Only the intervention of the Arts Council sustained the building through the 1980s, until its takeover and refurbishment under a charitable trust, which once again oversaw a successful populist programme with an emphasis on hit musicals. At the time I am about to find out 'what it is', *Miss Saigon* is playing to packed houses.

And since the old St. Mary's car park is lost to the new apartments, the audience's coaches and cars are now dispersed in various dead-end lanes that once served as loading bays for the nearby warehouses. The audience now filters in couples and small clusters towards the theatre doors from a quarter-mile radius around the theatre and in doing so are deflected into the path of the Petrol Liars, who, having established their marks' taste in schlock-fiction, are happy to provide an equally fantastical prelude or coda to the main event. It's not inevitable that the liars would be here, but for this moment the conditions in the city conspire to make their presence and their soliloquy possible:

'Scuse me. 'Scuse me. What it is mate, is that me car's broken
down near Tib Street. I'm sorry to bother you but I'm fucked for
getting home. I've got to look after me sister's kid. Her husband's

---

8 It was not uncommon for factory and warehouse workers to be paid in company-owned bars or music halls adjacent to the place of work and the company owned workers' cottages. Many literally accepted much of their wages in 'beer tokens' redeemable at these establishments.

on nights, he's got to get to work and it's her darts night tonight so she'll not hear her mobile. Me Mam never turns her phone on anyway and the battery's dead on mine even if she did (*gesture*), so I don't know what to do. I'll tell you what, though, mate. If you could just spare me a couple of pounds even, so I can get going I'm worried about my sister's kid. He's only nine and I've got to get back. Her husband'll be going mad and he's a big bastard and like I say, I'm really sorry to bother you but I'm just stuck and there it is. (*First breath.*) And I'm embarrassed to ask to tell you the truth, but seriously, if you give me your address I'll get it back to you and like, I don't know if you smoke like, but I can give you a little bit of this (*flash of what might be Oxo in cellophane*) . . . sorry, sorry, I'm embarrassed now, I just wanted to offer you something for your trouble. Can you please . . . just so I can get some petrol . . . Can you please help us out?

Fuckyethen₋tosser. (*Optional.*)

Disorientated, I hand over a pound, as much to get away as anything and begin the short walk back to my flat on the outskirts of the parking radius and the Petrol Liar's de facto invisible liberties.[9] For one reason or another it had been a difficult year for me and I was feeling disconnected from the city and my place in it. I'd been spending a lot of time alone in my flat and in my studio. The

---

9 It's embarrassing, but my first draft of this incident has me leaving the encounter seamlessly — describing the moment with a blithe detachment and the exchange of money as a knowing payment of 'mummer's rates' (after the travelling players and storytellers who once roamed the Irish countryside). The key being that I fooled myself into believing that I had framed the meeting through my own simultaneous interpretation and indulgence of an obvious lie, rather than retrospective justification of my actions. Seen from a distance of several years, several thousand miles and at the pace of my hacked typing, the latter account seems more accurate — and the lag, however infinitesimally small, between the moment and that consoling interpretation becomes a clearly measurable dimension of the con itself.

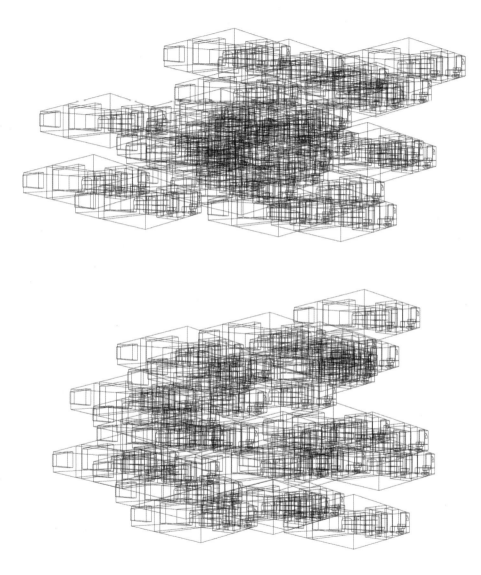

appeal from this man in the street was one of the few forms of sustained direct address I'd encountered that day and its sudden intensity and forced intimacy had animated the familiar street in an unexpected fashion.

Approaching the door of my building, I vaguely remembered the details of another one-on-one intervention — how in 1840s New York, a man frequenting Astor Place had given the world and his immediate neighbour Herman Melville the term 'Confidence Man'.[10] I loved that story. When I heard it, it seemed to tell me more about population density than any map or bare statistic would be capable of — something about a critical mass of per capita 'gullibility/alienation levels' being attained. A social shift that formed a rich vein to quietly mine with plausible plays on the mores of the time, and something that was mirrored now in the activities of the Mancunian Petrol Liars. Though, like the Confidence Man, whose grift became an idiomatic phrase,

---

10 'For the last few months a man has been traveling about the city, known as the "Confidence Man", that is, he would go up to a perfect stranger in the street, and being a man of genteel appearance, would easily command an interview. Upon this interview he would say after some little conversation, "have you confidence in me to trust me with your watch until tomorrow"; the stranger at this novel request, supposing him to be some old acquaintance not at that moment recollected, allows him to take the watch, thus placing "confidence" in the honesty of the stranger, who walks off laughing and the other supposing it to be a joke allows him so to do. In this way many have been duped, and the last that we recollect was a Mr. Thomas McDonald, of No. 276 Madison Street, who, on the 12th of May last, was met by this "Confidence Man" in William Street, who, in the manner as above described, took from him a gold lever watch valued at $110; and yesterday, singularly enough, Mr. McDonald was passing along Liberty Street, when who should he meet but the "Confidence Man" who had stolen his watch. Officer Swayse, of the Third Ward, being near at hand, took the accused into custody on the charge made by Mr. McDonald. The accused at first refused to go with the officer; but after finding the officer determined to take him, he walked along for a short distance, when he showed desperate fight, and it was not until the officer had tied his hands together that he was able to convey him to the police office. On the prisoner being taken before Justice McGrath, he was recognized as an old offender by the name of Wm. Thompson, and is said to be a graduate of the college at Sing Sing. The magistrate committed him to prison for a further hearing. It will be well for all those persons who have been defrauded by the "Confidence Man" to call at the police court Tombs and take a view of him.' (*New York Herald*, 1849)

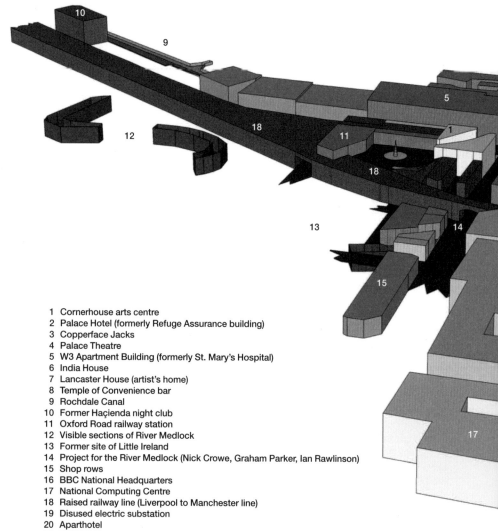

1   Cornerhouse arts centre
2   Palace Hotel (formerly Refuge Assurance building)
3   Copperface Jacks
4   Palace Theatre
5   W3 Apartment Building (formerly St. Mary's Hospital)
6   India House
7   Lancaster House (artist's home)
8   Temple of Convenience bar
9   Rochdale Canal
10 Former Haçienda night club
11 Oxford Road railway station
12 Visible sections of River Medlock
13 Former site of Little Ireland
14 Project for the River Medlock (Nick Crowe, Graham Parker, Ian Rawlinson)
15 Shop rows
16 BBC National Headquarters
17 National Computing Centre
18 Raised railway line (Liverpool to Manchester line)
19 Disused electric substation
20 Aparthotel
21 Exit

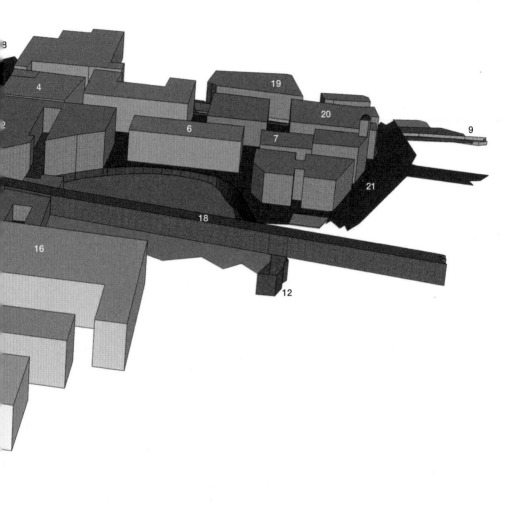

the latter's new nickname suggests that maybe the mining wasn't being done 'quietly' enough.

I was through the front door of my building now — debating whether to detour and pick up my mail in the post room. The post room was a depressing affair coated in discarded pizza menus and Council tax bills for ex-occupants. Every visit to it was prefaced with a pause and a moment of indecision. I'd lived in the flat since 1994 — the same year I'd built my first website. The post room was perhaps the first part of the physical world to 'fray' in my defaulting to a sub-jectivity informed by electronic settings — the first place where the metaphors borrowed from the physical world to describe cyberspace began to be unevenly mapped back in my gaze on the world. Aside from the fact that most of my bills were now being paid online and that e-mails had now superseded phone calls, let alone letters, as the principal method of random long-time-no-see messages from friends, the post room was awkward to get to. It was accessed by an electronic key fob and then through two doors that took me out of my way whether I was enter-ing or leaving the building. I'd come to think of it like the bulk mail folder in my e-mail program — somewhere where communications that had passed through rules-based filters ended up. Maintained, but barely worthy of regard. Somewhere to be checked in case something ended up there 'by mistake'.

It was hardly a responsible attitude but at some point there had definitely been a virtual concession of this space on my part and one that definitely bor-rowed from my growing involvement with online experience. Days could pass without me picking up my post, whilst on the other hand the once otherworldly and distressed sound of the dial-up modem was no longer a noteworthy phe-nomon in the wash of daily auditory experience.

BEDAWNG BEDAWNG

HOCCCCCCCCCCCCHHHHHHHHHH

SSSSSSSSSSSSSSSHHHHHHHHHHHHHHHHH

OCCCCCCCHHH.

KUP.

I skip the post room and head upstairs. There's a new e-mail from Bill Gates promising me money for forwarding this message.[11] It seems to still be light outside even though it's around 10 PM, though, given the narrowness of the streets and the position of my desk, I can't see the sky, just the building across the street that this week seems to be an apart-hotel boasting Internet access in each room. The serially cursed restaurant slot in its basement is currently a Chinese buffet – the Mongolian shield venture having failed to take off. From

---

11 A classic mid-1990s chain-mail spam where the mail recipient was encouraged to forward an e-mail to as many people as possible, allegedly as the trace element in a Microsoft exercise tracking worldwide patterns of e-mail usage. Enough forwards would supposedly trigger a payment from the company. Arguably, there was no real victim in this spam, other than the network itself being laid open to a pyramid-style multiplication of traffic, which is never without bandwidth cost. Anecdotal evidence at the time gave clues to the recurrent potency of the scam – partly fuelled by the apparently unstoppable trajectory of Microsoft's monopoly (and therefore the share of the riches suggested to participants) and partly by a persistent human vanity and gullibility that all scams depend upon to some degree. I spoke to a number of people at the time who, even when presented with evidence of this message's similarity to long-exposed chain mail scams, would insist that a friend of their brother had had a payout for taking part. David Maurer spoke of a similar response to wire and rag frauds in *The Big Con*, where fleeced victims would be dimly aware that there was a trick involved in their losing money in elaborate stings but in denial about the fact that they were the target of the trick. Maurer recounts victims approaching the very con artists who'd taken their fortunes and asking if they might try another hand at whatever 'game' they'd been inveigled into – repeating the fatal mistake of believing the scheme to be something free-standing, fairly assessable and beatable, when of course it was structured and adjusted to play perfectly on the blind spot of their self-justifying greed and belief in easy money.

12 The ironically named Temple of Convenience is a small bar housed in the unpromising subterranean setting of a former public toilet. Popular Manchester rumour had it that the toilet, located beside the one-time site of the Long Bar (a notorious gay haunt in the pre-legalisation days of the late 1940s and early 1950s) had been the site of the cruising arrest that led to Alan Turing's 'chemical castration' and ultimate suicide by ingestion of an apple dipped in cyanide. This version of Turing's arrest was not true. Neither was the claim that the Apple Mac logo was a nod to his suicide – though the influence he had on the philosophy of com-

the window I can just make out a sliver of one of the 92 locks of the
Rochdale canal behind the building. It has recently been cleaned up — part of
the alibi for the latest civic claim for what the city might be used for. The canal
runs beneath The Palace Theatre and Oxford Street, behind the W3 apartments, near the Temple of Convenience[12] and the closed Haçienda[13] nightclub
and into Castlefield basin near Liverpool Road, where the first inter-city passen-
ger train had arrived in Manchester on September 15, 1830.[14] The canals

---

putational thought was undoubtedly immense and it would not have been beyond the realm
of possibility for him to have been acknowledged in this kind of hacker in-joke. Nor would it
have been beyond the realm of possibility for a clandestine sexual encounter involving
Turing to have taken place at what is now the Temple of Convenience. Whatever the apoc-
ryphal origins of his link to this particular site, several queer theorists have noted that the
pre- and post-legalisation sexuality of the city had long involved an elaborate rereading and
delinquent repurposing of the architectural and communication structures of the ware-
housed city centre (records exist of nineteenth-century warehouse owners painting alcove
doors with pitch at weekends to deter opportunistic couples) long before the moment of loft
conversions and gay warehouse bars leading Manchester's 1990s revival. The canals were
key in this — neglected sites that failed to function and signify correctly in the declining
moments of the industrial city, they became sites for encounters and escape routes from
those encounters — liberties of a sort (in that they belonged to the city but were no longer
functionally 'of' it). Networks to be hacked.

13 A former yacht showroom turned post-industrial flagship for Factory Records, named after a
quote in a Situationist text: 'And you . . . without music and without geography, no longer setting out for the haçienda . . . That's all over. You'll never see the haçienda. It doesn't exist.
The haçienda must be built' (Ivan Chtcheglov, *Formulary for a New Urbanism*, 1953).
Manchester pop culture's relationship to Situationism is an interesting ongoing exercise in
misunderstanding, recuperation and idealism that, for better or worse, runs like a mineral
seam through most reasonably thorough accounts of the city's recent cultural life. As the
Chtcheglov text goes on to say, 'All cities are geological. You can't take three steps without
encountering ghosts bearing all the prestige of their legends.' Factory, run by the late Tony
Wilson, was always astute about enhancing its own legend whilst publicly disavowing the his-
toricising that increasingly underwrites that legend. In this it had something in common with
the Petrol Liar in that it proposed extravagant claims about its circumstances yet actively cam-
paigned against scrutiny of those claims.

themselves had been built on the type of extravagant rhetoric that Nicholas Negroponte and *Wired* had recently used to talk about the information revolution (in the more historical case, the 'blinding-with-science' involved the engineering genius James Brindley demonstrating the function of an aqueduct with the aid of a model made from round cheese and sculpting raw clay in the parliamentary committee room to demonstrate his innovative, non-leaking, 'puddling' technique to sceptical government ministers).

In some ways it could be argued that the canals were a curious false start in the Industrial Revolution in Britain. Although extensive canal networks ran through

---

14 Also the date of the first rail fatality, when the member of Parliament for Liverpool, William Huskisson, misjudged the speed of the advancing Rocket train and was run over whilst standing on the line talking to the then Prime Minister, the Duke of Wellington, through an open carriage window. The train continued to Manchester, where the Duke, in an unrelated incident having more to do with his economic policies, was pelted with bricks. The Liverpool–Manchester route was also distinctive for an indeterminate management structure in its early years, which threatened to bring chaos to the line – mostly prompted by the Liverpool–Manchester Act, which offered a novel organic approach to infrastructural development: 'Gustave Cohn notes that a clause of the Liverpool–Manchester Act guarantees free access to all vehicles: "All persons shall have free liberty to use with carriages all roads, ways and passages for the purpose of conveying goods or passengers or cattle . . . For this to be possible, the carriages used by the freight entrepreneurs have to conform to those regulations that the railroad company deems practicable and advertises in every station. Furthermore the owners of adjoining property receive the right to construct branch lines to the Liverpool–Manchester line"' (Wolfgang Schivelbusch, *The Railway Journey*, 1979). Schivelbusch adds that as late as 1838 there were still private vehicles on the Liverpool–Manchester line – a vestige of the liberal economic policies that governed turnpikes and canals, but which had somewhat more problematic implications on a fixed-track railway line . . .

15 This was not so much the case in America, where the ontological leap made in most people's minds was that of waterway to railway. The very location of major cities there had hitherto been determined by proximity to natural or man-made waterways and for a significant period of time everything from camber to sleeping layouts to mean speed of locomotives drew a cue from the water-based transport that had preceded the railways (particularly the steamers, or 'floating palaces', one of which was to provide the setting for Melville's *The Confidence-Man*). Right up to the 1860s the average long distance American railroad journey took place at a speed around half that of its European counterpart, for no apparent technological reason than the journey's origins in

major cities in the country, the popular ontological segue that took place to bring the trains to prominence was largely from stagecoach to train rather than from waterway to train.[15] In modern-day Manchester the canals have come to be the guidelines for redevelopment and new buildings — their presence on the street maps is certainly prominent and consistent compared to, say, the River Medlock, upon which the city was founded but whose present visibility and representation within the iconography of the city is intermittent at best.[16]

Anyway, I can glimpse the canal, beyond which lies the blank wall of an electricity substation. I can hear the sound of the street beneath me though I can't

river transport. Unlike the compartment-bound, stagecoach-like European journey, though, the American train experience came to be modelled on the aim of an open, self-sustaining 'palace on wheels'. The following lines from Foucault's description of ocean travel could equally apply to the intensity of the American dream of the railway: 'if we think, after all, that the boat is a floating piece of space, a place without a place, that exists by itself, that is closed in on itself and at the same time is given over to the infinity of the sea and that, from port to port, from tack to tack, from brothel to brothel, it goes as far as the colonies in search of the most precious treasures they conceal in their gardens, you will understand why the boat has not only been for our civilization, from the sixteenth century until the present, the great instrument of economic development . . . but has been simultaneously the greatest reserve of the imagination. The ship is the heterotopia par excellence. In civilizations without boats, dreams dry up, espionage takes the place of adventure, and the police take the place of pirates. (Michel Foucault, 'Of Other Spaces', 1967)

16 The rivers and the terrain of Manchester were the subject of four significant projects in a five-year period for me. In *Mugger Music* (made as a member of index co-operative in collaboration with Ian Rawlinson, 1996), the River Medlock was used as an alternative route in a series of city centre walks repeated every half-hour for 24 hours by three guides working in relay — each accompanying one ticket-buying member of the public. In that work the walkers would intersect with the burgeoning 24-hour economy (shops, hotels, snooker centres, artists' studios) at the points where the river's presence had been actively occluded — its indifferent constancy set against the policed vigilance of 2:30 AM Manchester or the abandoned streets of 4 PM Manchester on FA cup-final day (Manchester United were playing arch rivals Liverpool). The work was later adapted for Lower Manhattan (1997). In *Project for the River Medlock* (in collaboration with Nick Crowe and Ian Rawlinson, 1998), the intersection of the road, rail and river systems was marked by an intervention in which three steel panels painted in a mural were replaced by three sheets of toughened glass on a bridge overlooking the river, and a set of loudspeakers would automatically amplify the volume of the river according to the volume of

see the source of the voices. There's a frayed quality to the soundscape, though
– a signal that the well-heeled theatregoers are giving way to the weekend rev-
ellers, changing venues from pub to club as closing time approaches. I think of
the Petrol Liar again – think of his main constituency slipping through his fin-
gers for the night, drunks being as likely to turn belligerent as sentimental. Bad
for business to create a scene.

On an urge I head away from the window and leave the door, passing the
source of the only light in the room – the blue-white glow from the mail inbox
on the oatmeal-coloured monitor that takes up half the desk. I leave the flat
and jog down the fire exit stairs, hitting the street by the fake Irish bar. Sure
enough, my target has moved up the street and is about to round the corner.
He is purposeful – brisk and taut. His body language is utterly transformed,
as is mine (largely by a new weight of narrative self-consciousness that makes
me acutely aware of my proximity to others and the consistency and purpose

---

the ambient surroundings (i.e., when a bus went past on Oxford Road or a train went over-
head). In *Square City* (2000), I was commissioned as 'artist-in-residence' in the 1 km Ordnance
Survey grid square where I lived (84E97N on the Manchester map). For a year I carried out
various audits, interventions and surveys within the square (the most successful of which, in
retrospect, were barely publicly visible), such as recording and transcribing the drunks outside
my flat each Saturday night at midnight to track the moments when certain popular songs left
a particular collective memory ('Who Let the Dogs Out?' peaked and disappeared that year),
or patrolling the arbitrary perimeters of the square on foot. In *End Users* (2001), a solo show at
the Centre for the Understanding of the Built Environment, I gathered the user dictionaries
(an automatically generated document listing words a user has asked the computer to learn
during spell checks) from several hundred architects' computers in Manchester and compiled
them into a single composite text that ran around the walls of the gallery in a single unbroken
line. This project was as revealing for its absences as it was for its collection of place names,
local idioms and technical jargon – the user dictionaries I gathered from several local artists,
musicians and writers at the same time revealed several mentions of Guy Debord (see p.17, fn.
13), who was entirely absent from the architects' list. As per my initial response to the Petrol
Liar (see p.8, fn. 9), I would love to think that this heightened state of surveillance and playful
sense of ownership made me less susceptible to the con on 'my' turf, but if anything it just
opened a different pocket.

of the people on the street — without being entirely sure what I'm looking for — a nod to Poe's frustrated narrator in 'The Man of the Crowd ').[17] In his case, where our encounter was based on an intimate forestalling of every possible step away from him (a claustrophobia induced in the victim by a quick degree of practised physical and verbal blocking), he is now at pains to prevent any such intrusion being practised on him in turn and is arrowing straight through the small packs of drunks with only the barest shifts to avoid clashing shoulders. He is visibly on his toes, whereas our initial encounter presented the illusory appearance of him being on his heels — even as he had consistently shifted weight to ensure the privacy and continuation of my audience with him, in true rope-a-dope style.

As he turns onto Princess Street, I have an urge to catch up and speak with him — perhaps seeking some classic mark's reassurance that it was nothing personal, that I know the score, that I understand the potential of this street, this city, this network, too. It's a brief thought and tinged with a feeling of betrayal — even though I'd prided myself on seeing the transparency of his lie straight away, I'd allowed the fiction to unfold through to his sought-after outcome, and here he was leaving the ritual without a bow, in open disdain for his audience. And as I watch, he adds a final comic insult by climbing into a white hatchback car driven by an accomplice, and they drive off without looking back.

A pause. I try to look as purposeful as my absent target and spin round comically on the street to head back to my flat, adding a genuine half-skip of urgency as I remember that I'd left the dial-up connection open. I am taken aback by my own susceptibility to the dual levels of the con — not so much the crude mechanics of the trick itself as the concurrent play on my belief that spot-

---

17 '"The old man," I said at length, "is the type and the genius of deep crime. He refuses to be alone. He is the man of the crowd. It will be in vain to follow, for I shall learn no more of him, nor of his deeds."' (Edgar Allan Poe, *The Man of the Crowd*, 1840)

ting those mechanics made me somehow exempt from being victim to them —
a classic victim's vanity. The con had taken place when I'd legitimised the intervention in the first place — privileging that voice and that agenda out of the hun-
dreds on the street. The content was perhaps incidental — I'd sold myself to it
already. It is what it is.

ILLUSTRATIONS

FRONT AND BACK COVER *Short Con*, Graham Parker, 2006. From a series of neon signs based on titles of spam e-mails.

INSIDE FRONT AND BACK COVER *+Turing +Apple* (detail), Graham Parker, Giclée print, 46" x 34", 2006.

PAGE 5 *Barnum* (detail), Graham Parker, 35 mm slides, 2000, cf. *Spectres of Marks*, p. 17.

PAGE 10 *If you want to get there, I wouldn't start from here*, Graham Parker, Giclée print, 2000. Composite drawings made from daily GPS satellite readings from device held out of artist's window during Square City project (see p. 19, fn. 16). The drawings plotted the apparent relative positions of the flat due to reading fluctuations caused by cloud cover, the proximity of the buildings on the Victorian street and the built-in margin of error on reported satellite positions imposed by the U.S. military, who had developed the technology. The latter variable was removed on April 1, 2000 — ushering in the technological and ideological potential of the age of locative media.

PAGES 12 AND 13 *Central Manchester,* Graham Parker, annotated animation still, 2008.

PAGE 14 *End Users* (installation views), Graham Parker, 2001. Installation at Centre for the Understanding of the Built Environment. See p. 19, fn. 16.

PAGE 23 *Untitled,* Jim Medway, colour photograph, 1997.

All other illustrations, Graham Parker, 2008.